MARKETING YOUR WAY TO EASY LIVING

Eight Ways to Market Your Small Business
to the Masses

David L. McKimmy

WestBow
PRESS
A DIVISION OF THOMAS NELSON

WestBow Press books may be ordered through booksellers or by contacting:

WestBow Press
A Division of Thomas Nelson
1663 Liberty Drive
Bloomington, IN 47403
www.westbowpress.com
1-(866) 928-1240

Because of the dynamic nature of the Internet, any web addresses or links contained in this book may have changed since publication and may no longer be valid. The views expressed in this work are solely those of the author and do not necessarily reflect the views of the publisher, and the publisher hereby disclaims any responsibility for them.

Any people depicted in stock imagery provided by Thinkstock are models, and such images are being used for illustrative purposes only.

Certain stock imagery © Thinkstock.

ISBN: 978-1-4497-3669-9 (hbk)
ISBN: 978-1-4497-3667-5 (sc)
ISBN: 978-1-4497-3668-2 (e)
Library of Congress Control Number: 2012900958

Printed in the United States of America

WestBow Press rev. date: 01/31/2012

Table of Contents

Dedication

I would like to dedicate my first book to my spouse, Darlene. I admire your hard work and creativity you put toward your own small business. You are a true success and the hardest-working person I know. A huge thank-you to my daughter, Leighanne, for your understanding of the time it takes to write a book and believing in me, with all the words of encouragement. I hope I make you just as proud as you have made me! I believe family is one's only true indispensible asset.

I would also like to thank all of the great people I've come into contact with over the years. They have shaped my thought process and techniques I now teach others. I believe your success is measured in the number of friends you collect over your lifetime.

Thanks to the many sales coaches I've listened to on tape and whose books I've devoured: Zig Ziglar, Bryan Tracy, Earl Nightingale, Tony Robbins, and so on. These are books and tapes I still revisit. I believe you can never learn enough.

To all of you—thank you!

David

P.S. Remember, rich people buy books and businesses; others buy things!

Introduction

When I put pen to paper, or keyboard to Word document, I found myself with an enormous amount of useful marketing material I've used since 1992. This experience is drawn from many business positions, including sales manager for a small Midwest manufacturing firm; owner and manager of three restaurants; owner of a restaurant equipment and supply company; owner() of a small business consulting company(www.salescoachpro.com); financial services and insurance company and an e-commerce website(www.ubuyrite.com). Several of these I continue to own but consult from afar. The strategies I talk about in this book are still in place in these companies. By mastering the principles I share in this book, I have found starting and getting a business off the ground remarkably easy.

Even though I truly believe we are all one or two great marketing ideas away from more sales opportunities than we can fully imagine, I believe the first two chapters are as important as the following eight. The strategies in this book—when implemented with conviction and care—are guaranteed to make you more money with less effort. These are strategies that have helped businesses just like yours; including your competitors, make hundreds of thousands of dollars.

This is why I have dedicated my life to business consulting. Since starting my company that provides direction for small business operators, I have been overwhelmed with the demand for marketing and structure, and the need for someone who provides a proper third-party perspective.

As you read the principles to follow, remember it does not matter what industry or type of business you operate (I've been part of many). What matters is that you grasp the heart of the principles, the underlying lessons and strategies, that can help grow any operation in any category of business.

The best time to start is *now*—not tomorrow, not next week, not next year.

Yours in success,

David L. McKimmy

P.S. If you would like to arrange a meeting to get a third-party, profitable perspective on your business, please e-mail Salescoachpro.com, and we will gladly point you in the right direction.

For a free test drive of all my best tips, tricks, and marketing resources, visit www.SalesCoachPro.com.

1

Using Goal-Setting Effectively

We've all heard about the power of setting goals. Everyone has surely seen statistics that connect goal-setting to success in both your business life and your personal life. I'm sure if I asked you today what your goals are, you could rattle off a few wants and hopes without thinking too long.

However, what most people do not realize is that the power of goal-setting lies in *writing down your goals.* I believe, committing goals to paper and reviewing them regularly gives you a a far higher chance of achieving your desired outcomes. I believe only a very small percentage of people in the world have written goals—I believe this same small percentage achieve greater success in business and earn considerable wealth.

Having said that, a vast majority, in my opinion, will NOT have enough saved to sustain their lifestyle at retirement age. As a business owner, it is essential that you develop a plan for your retirement. It is equally essential that you develop a plan for your success.

This chapter focuses on the power of goal-setting as part of your business success. I'll teach you to set SMART goals that are rooted in your own personal value system and supporting techniques to achieve your goals faster.

What Are Goals?

Goals are clear targets that are attached to a specific time frame and action plan. They focus your efforts and drive your motivation in a clear direction. Goals are different from dreams in that they outline a plan of action, while dreams are a conceptual vision of your wish or desired outcome.

Goals require work: work on yourself, work for your business, and work for others. You cannot achieve a goal—no matter how badly you want it—without being prepared to make a considerable effort. If you are ready to invest your time and energy, goals will help you

> realize a dream or wish for your personal or business life,
> make a change in your life (add positive influences or remove negative ones),
> improve your skills and performance ability, and
> start or change a habit (positive or negative).

Why Set Goals?

As we've already reviewed, setting goals and committing them to paper is the most effective way to cultivate success. The most important reason to set a goal *is to attach a clear action plan to a desired outcome.*

Goals help focus our time and energy on one (or several) key outcome at a time. Many business owners have hundreds of ideas, as well as daily responsibilities, whirring around in their heads at any one time. By writing down and focusing on a few ideas at a time, you can prioritize and concentrate your efforts, avoid being stretched too thin, and produce greater results.

Since goals attach action to outcomes, goals can help break big dreams into manageable and achievable sections. Creating a multi-goal strategy will put a road map in place to help you get to your desired outcome. If your goal is to start a pizza business and make six figures a year, there are a number of smaller steps to achieve before reaching your end result.

Success doesn't happen by itself. It is the result of consistent and committed action by an individual who is driven to achieve something. Success means something different for everyone, so creating goals is a personal endeavor. Goals can be large and small, personal and public, financial and spiritual. It is not the size of the goal that matters; what matters is that you write down the goal and commit to making the effort required to achieve it.

What Happens When I Achieve a Goal?

You should congratulate yourself and your team, of course! By rewarding yourself and your team after every achievement, you not only train your mind to associate hard work with reward but also develop loyalty among your employees.

You should also ask yourself if your achievement can be taken to the next level or if your goal can be stretched by building on the effort you have already made. Consistently setting new and higher targets will lay the framework for constant improvement and personal and professional growth.

The Power of Positive Thinking

When was the last time you tuned in to your internal stream of consciousness? What does the stream of thoughts that runs through your mind sound like? Are your thoughts positive? Negative? Are they logical? Reasonable?

Positive thinking and healthy self-talk are the most important business tools you can ever cultivate. By programming a positive stream of subconscious thoughts into your mind, you can control your reality and, ultimately, your goals. Think about someone you know who is constantly negative—someone who complains, whines, and makes excuses for his or her unhappiness. How successful is that person? How do his or her fears and doubts become reality in the world?

You are what you continuously believe about yourself and your environment. If you focus your mind on something in your mental world, it will nearly always manifest as reality in your physical world. Positive thinking is a key part of setting goals. You won't achieve your goal until you believe you can. You will achieve your goals faster when you believe in yourself and those around you who are helping to make your goal a reality.

Successful people are rooted in a strong belief system—belief in themselves, the work they are doing, and the people around them. They are motivated to improve and learn but also confident in their existing skills and knowledge. Their positive attitudes and energy are clearly felt in everything they do.

Do you ever notice how complainers usually surround themselves with other complainers? The same is true of positive thinkers. If you cultivate an upbeat and positive attitude, you will be surrounded by people who share your values and outlook on life.

Too often, people in our society subscribe to a continuous stream of negative chatter. The more you hear it, the more you'll believe it. How many times have you heard the following phrases?

- That's impossible.
- Don't even bother.
- It's already been done.
- We tried that, and it didn't work.
- You're too young.

- You're too old.
- You'll never get there.
- You'll never get that done.
- You can't do that.

Positive thinking and positive influences will provide the support you need to achieve your goals. Choose your friends and close colleagues wisely, and surround yourself with positive thinkers.

Creating SMART Goals

SMART goals are just that—smart. Whether you are setting goals for your personal life, your business, or with your employees, goals that have been developed using the SMART principle, in my opinion, have a higher probability of being achieved.

The SMART principle is

1. Specific

Specific goals are clearer and easier to achieve than nonspecific ones. When writing down your goal, ask yourself the five W questions—Who? What? When? Where? Why?—to narrow down what you are aiming to achieve.

For example, instead of a nonspecific goal, like, "Get in shape for the summer," a specific goal would be, "Go to the gym three times a week, and eat twice as many vegetables."

2. Measurable

If you can't measure your goal, how will you know when you've achieved it? Measurable goals help you clearly see where you are and where you want to be. You can see change as it happens.

Measurable goals can also be broken down and managed in smaller pieces. They make it easier to create an action plan or identify the steps required to achieve your goal. You can track your progress, revise your plan, and celebrate each small achievement. For example, instead of aiming to increase revenue in 2011, you can set out to increase revenue by 30 percent in the next twelve months and celebrate each 10 percent increase along the way.

3. Achievable

Goals that are achievable have a higher chance of being realized. While it is important to think big and dream big, too often people set goals that are simply beyond their capabilities, so they wind up disappointed. Goals can stretch you, but they should always be feasible to maintain your motivation and commitment.

For example, if you want to complete your first triathlon but you've never run a mile in your life, you would be setting a goal that was beyond your current capabilities. If you decided instead to train for a five-mile race in six months, you would be setting an achievable goal.

4. Relevant

Relevant or realistic goals have a logical place in your life or overall business strategy. The goal's action plan can be reasonably integrated into your life with a realistic amount of effort.

For example, if your goal is to train to climb to base camp at Mount Everest within one year and you're about to launch a start-up business, you may need to question the relevance of your goal in the context of your current commitments.

5. Timely

It is essential for every goal to be attached to a time frame; otherwise, it is merely a dream. Make sure your time frame is realistic—not too short or too long. This will keep you motivated and committed to your action plan and allow you track your progress.

Autosuggestion + Visualization

Autosuggestion and visualization are two techniques that can assist you in achieving your goals. I believe some of the most well-known and successful people in the world use these techniques, and it is not coincidence they are masters in their own fields of business and sport. A few of these people are as follows:

- Michael Phelps (Olympic swimmer)
- Andre Agassi (tennis player)
- Donald Trump (real estate developer)

- Wayne Gretzky (hockey player)
- Bill Gates (Microsoft cofounder)
- Walt Disney (entertainment executive)

Of course, each of these people had a high degree of talent, ambition, intelligence, and drive. However, to reach the top of their respective fields, they each used autosuggestion and visualization.

Autosuggestion

Autosuggestion is your internal dialogue: the constant stream of thoughts and comments that flows through your mind, and impacts what you think about yourself and how you perceive situations. Go to YouTube and search "Donald Trump," and you will see this in action.

Since you were a small child, this self-talk has been influenced by your experiences and has programmed your mind to think and react in certain ways. The good news is that you can reprogram your mind and customize your self-talk in any way you like. That is the power of autosuggestion.

To begin practicing autosuggestion, make sure you are relaxed and open to trying the technique. An ideal time is just before bed or when you have some time to sit quietly. Then, repeat positive affirmations to yourself about the ideal outcome. Top sports and businesspeople will often practice just before a big game or meeting.

Some examples of positive self-talk or autosuggestion include the following:

- I will lead my team to a victory tonight.
- I will be relaxed and open to meeting new people at the party tonight.
- I will deliver a clear and impacting speech.
- I will stop worrying and tackle this problem tomorrow.
- I will stand up for my own ideas in the meeting.
- I will remember everything I have studied for the test tomorrow.

Visualization

Visualization is a complementary practice to autosuggestion. While you can repeat affirmations to yourself over and over, combining this practice with visualization makes the affirmations twice as powerful.

Visualization is exactly what it sounds like: repeatedly visualizing in your mind's eye how something is going to happen. Nearly everyone in sports practices this technique. This should prove to enhance performance better than practice alone.

This technique can easily be applied to business. For example, use visualization prior to any presentation or meeting where you must speak, present, or "perform." You can also visualize yourself being incredibly productive and effective in your office. Or, in your personal life, visualize having a calm and rational discussion with your spouse. (I do this all the time, especially before meeting with an important prospect)

Elements to think about during visualization:

- What does the room look like?
- What do people in the room look like?
- What is their mood? How do they receive me?
- What image do I project?
- How do I look?
- How do I behave? What is my attitude?
- What is the outcome?

2

Systemizing Your Business and Developing Effective Processes

If you want the rewards every business owner truly deserves, you must make the time to work on your business instead of in it. For many people, this is easier said than done. The majority of business owners tend to operate in a reactive mode; that is, they are constantly focused on the day-to-day operations rather than the long-term strategic growth of their business.

In order to find the time to work strategically on growing the business, it is vital business owners look at every possible way they can begin to systematize their operations. This chapter explores ways systems can be implemented and used to ensure a healthy, profitable, and sustainable business, regardless of whether the owner is actually involved in the day-to-day operations.

What Is a System?

Put simply, a system is something that does not rely on human beings. In other words, it is something that can operate independently of people, even though people originally created it. A system can be a sign, a banner, an audiotape or videotape, an inquiry register, a "how-to" manual, or a laminated set of instructions.

Why Do I Need Systems?

There are many reasons why every business should be focused on becoming system based:

- Systems make sure you don't forget opportunities.
- Systems allow you to avoid unnecessary costs.
- Systems save you time.
- Systems reassure staff and customers.
- Systems create desired behaviors and outcomes.
- Systems help you focus on long-term strategic objectives.
- Systems let you maximize all available sales opportunities.
- Systems let you develop better negotiation and persuasion techniques.
- Systems will improve prospecting efforts.

- Systems will allow you to improve the quality of your staff training.
- Systems will allow you to become a more effective leader.

In short, systems are key to operating a successful business in today's highly competitive marketplace.

How Do I Create Systems?

The first step in creating systems in your business is to analyze everything you and your staff do on a daily basis. The best way to do this is to use a daily journal you can find at any office supply store. The daily journal lets you break down all the day's activities into fifteen-minute segments. You can then prioritize each activity on a scale of 1 to 10, with 10 being highly relevant and the most important. Once you have done this on a regular basis, you will start to see patterns of behavior emerge. These are certain duties or chores that need to be carried out on a regular basis. It is often among these duplicated tasks that your first opportunities to start systematizing will be found.

An example

Many business owners find themselves in a reactive mode throughout their working day, because they are always available to answer questions or help staff members solve problems. While this is important, it can also be an unproductive use of the owner's time. A simple system to avoid this is to allocate two periods of the day where you, as the business owner, are available to answer these questions. If someone has an issue or question, they write it down in a "question registry," which you will attend to twice a day. Make sure there is space available next to the question for them to write down what the person thinks the answer is. This will make people start to think through the issue, and invariably, many people will be able to solve the problem themselves. If they can't, you can start to see how your staff deals with problem solving and the areas you need to focus on in terms of increased training.

So, by using this simple system,

- you become more productive,
- your staff begin to appreciate your time more,
- you have a written list of common problems or issues to deal with on a daily basis,
- your staff will now start to think things through more effectively, and
- you can now identify areas for further training and improvement.

The second step to installing systems in your business is to document every new system and experiment with staff, suppliers, and customers. It is also very important to revise where and when necessary and make refinements. It is unlikely you will create the perfect system every time, so it is important to review your systems regularly to make sure they remain effective. Putting together a company binder with all these systems will help. Many systems, such as the examples that follow, are easy to implement.

Staff Uniforms

Uniforms help to systematize attire and presentation. Many people either don't know how or don't care about presenting themselves in the best possible light. This is why having all of your team dress the same way is important. For example, my wife is a Dentist and when she first started her practice, the staff was allowed to dress in any color scrub they wanted. Well, as you can imagine, they looked disorganized, which gave the perception the business was being run poorly. My wife, also dressed in scrubs, confused the new patients on who was the Doctor. She made a change, and the employees all dress in the same colored scrubs, and she wears nice clothes under her clinical jacket, so no mistaking who the Doctor is. By having coordination and proper attire by my wife and staff, this takes away the opportunity for her patients to judge her organization by the way they're dressed.

Sales Scripts

Making sure your company's product presentation is scripted makes a lot of sense. This is not to say that everyone should provide standard robotic questions and answers or not be allowed to inject his or her own personality, but in the all-important area of presenting your products and services, it is important everyone says what you want said, your way, every time.

Having the answers to common objections laminated and within easy reach will ensure that your staff are able to handle comfortably any potential customer objections. It will also ensure a smooth, flowing exchange that culminates in an easier sale. Scripting both inbound and outbound telemarketing calls is an absolute must, unless you are a very talented telemarketer. And even then, it's still a good idea. Having a structured process for handling customer complaints is also crucial.

Form Letters

Having and using a set of standard letters personalized for your business is a very simple system that can save you a lot of time and potential embarrassment. In my coaching site, www.salescoachpro.com, there is a detailed section on how to write effective sales letters, with many examples you can modify for your own business.

Contact Logs

Any business that receives inbound client inquiries should create an contact log. This can be on your computer or in a ledger-style book format. Businesses lose so many potential sales because they don't record every inbound inquiry.

When you calculate what you spend every year on all of your advertising and marketing programs, you will quickly realize those incoming inquiries are golden. So many people forget that every phone call received has the potential to cost—as well as make—them money.

You must record all of the relevant information, including where the caller got your number and what was said to the caller. It is also vital to have a follow-up procedure to see what became of the inquiry and, if you lost the business, why you lost it. If you are truly serious about building your business to a new level, you should keep all of these inquiries in a separate file on your database for future follow-up. People respect persistence, and if you stay in contact when everyone else can't be bothered, you will win in the long run.

Workflow Procedures

Setting up systems to ensure smooth-flowing administration procedures can not only provide better efficiencies but can also dramatically cut business costs. One of the most effective ways to analyze workflow procedures is to stand back from what you know and are comfortable with and start asking, "Why?" Why do you do things the way that you do? Is it because, "That's the way it's always been done"? If that's the answer, you need to determine if there is a better way. One of the fastest ways to do this is to involve your staff (and even reward them!) for coming up with more efficient ways of doing things. It is amazing what you can learn by asking people for their input or opinion.

Systems will set you free.

When you begin the process of completely systematizing your business, customers will know what to expect every time, and staff will know what to do in every instance. Then, your need for active involvement is reduced. The following will also occur:

- Your business becomes more valuable.
- Your business becomes easier to sell.
- You will be better prepared to raise capital.
- You will be able to duplicate your business easily.
- You can factor more time into your personal life.
- Your business becomes a system for you to grow your wealth—not a job you do.

Putting together a binder of all these systems and giving one to each employee will keep things uniform. Any questions an employee may have should be found in this evolving manual. At the end of the day, most people like and need direction, such as that found in the company manual.

The next eight chapters focus on the core reason for picking up this book. Marketing is a key component of any great company—Gillette, Apple, Rolex, McDonalds, and so on. Please learn and master these next chapters. Your company bank account will thank you for it.

3

Defining Your Target Market

What Is a Target Market?

Many businesses can't answer the question, "Who is your target market?" They have often made the fatal assumption that, with the right marketing strategy, everyone will want to purchase their product or service.

A target market is simply the group of customers or clients who will purchase a specific product or service. This group has something in common, often age, gender, hobbies, or location. Your target market, then, are those who will buy what you offer. This includes both existing and potential customers, all of whom are motivated to do one of three things:

- fulfill a need
- solve a problem
- satisfy a desire

To build, maintain, and grow your business, you need to know who your customers are, what they do, what they like, and why they would buy your product or service. Getting this wrong will cost you time, money, and potentially the success of your business.

The Importance of Knowing Your Target Market

Knowledge and understanding of your target market is the keystone in the arch of your business. Without it, your product or service positioning, pricing, marketing strategy, and eventually your business could very quickly fall apart. If you don't intimately know your target market, you run the risk of making mistakes when it comes to establishing pricing, product mix, or service packages. Your marketing strategy will lack direction and produce mediocre results at best. Even if your marketing message is clear and your brochure is perfectly designed, it means nothing unless it arrives in the hands—or ears—of the right people.

Determining your target market takes time and careful diligence. While it often starts with a best guess, assumptions cannot be relied on, and research is required to confirm original ideas.

Once you build an understanding of who makes up your target market, keep up with your market research. Having your finger on the pulse of its motivations and drivers—which naturally change—will help you anticipate needs or wants and evolve your business.

Types of Markets

Consumer

The consumer market includes general consumers who buy products and services for personal use or for use by family and friends. This is the market category you or I fall into when we're shopping for groceries or clothes, seeing a movie in the theater, or going out for lunch. Retailers focus on this market category when marketing their goods or services.

Institutional

The institutional market provides products or services for the benefit of society. This includes hospitals, nonprofit organizations, government organizations, schools, and universities. Members of the institutional market purchase products to use in the provision of services to people in their care.

Business to Business (B2B)

The B2B market is just what it seems to be: businesses who purchase the products and services of other businesses to run their operations. These purchases can include products used to manufacture other products (raw or technical), products needed for daily operations (like office supplies), or services (like accounting, shredding, and legal).

Reseller

This market can also be called the "intermediary market," because it consists of businesses that act as channels for goods and services between other markets. Goods are purchased and sold for a profit—without any alterations. Members of this market include wholesalers, retailers, resellers, and distributors.

Determining Your Target Market

Product/Service Investigation

The process of determining your target market starts by examining exactly what you are offering and your average customer's motivation for purchasing it. Begin by answering the following questions:

Does your offering meet a basic need?	
Does your offering serve a particular want?	
Does your offering fulfill a desire?	
What is the life cycle of your product/service?	
What is the availability of your offering?	

What is the value of the average customer's purchase?	
How many times or how often will customers purchase your offering?	
Do you foresee any upcoming changes in your industry or region that may positively or negatively affect the sales of your offering?	

Market Investigation

- *On the ground.* Spend some time on the researching who your target market might be. If you're thinking about opening a coffee shop, hang out in the neighborhood at different times of the day to get a sense of the people who live, work, and play in that area.
- *The competition.* Who does your direct competitor target? Is there a small niche that is being missed? Observing your competition's clientele can help to build understanding of your target market, regardless of whether it is the same as or opposite that of your competition. For example, if you own a children's clothing boutique and the majority of middle-class mothers shop at the local department store, you may wish to focus on higher-income families as your target market.

- *Online.* Many cities and towns—or at least regions—have demographic information available online. Research the ages, incomes, occupations, and other key pieces of information about the people who live in the area where you operate your business. From this data, you will gain an understanding of the size of your total potential market.

- *Existing customers.* Talk to your existing customers through focus groups or surveys. This is a great way to gather demographic and behavioral information, as well as genuine feedback about product or service quality. You'll also obtain other types of information that will be useful in developing a business or marketing strategy.

Who Is Your Market?

Based on your product/service and market investigations, you will be able to piece together a basic picture of your target market and some of its general characteristics. Record some notes here. At this point, you may be as specific as possible or maintain some generalities. You can further segment your market in the next chapter.

Consumer Target Market Framework

Market Type:	Consumer	
Gender:	☐ Male	☐ Female
Age Range:		
Purchase Motivation:	☐ Meet a Need ☐ Serve a Want ☐ Fulfill a Desire	
Activities:		
Income Range:		
Marital Status:		
Location:	☐ Neighborhood ☐ City ☐ Region ☐ Country	
Other Notes:		

Institutional Target Market Framework

Market Type:	Institutional
Institution Type:	☐ Hospital ☐ Nonprofit ☐ School ☐ University ☐ Charity ☐ Government ☐ Church
Purchase Motivation:	
Purchase Motivation:	☐ Operational Need ☐ Client Need ☐ Client Desire
Purpose of Institution:	
Institution's Client Base:	
Size:	
Location:	☐ Neighborhood ☐ City ☐ Region ☐ Country
Other Notes:	

B2B Target Market Framework

Market Type:	Business to Business (B2B)
Company Size:	
Number of Employees:	
Purchase Motivation:	☐ Operations Need ☐ Strategy ☐ Functionality
Annual Revenue:	
Industry:	
Location(s):	
Purpose of Business:	
People, Culture, and Values:	
Other Notes:	

Reseller Target Market Framework

Market Type:	Reseller
Industry:	
Client Base:	
Purchase Motivation:	☐ Operations Need ☐ Client Wants ☐ Functionality
Annual Revenue:	
Age:	
Location:	☐ Neighborhood ☐ City ☐ Region ☐ Country
Other Notes:	

Your Target Market: Putting It Together

Based on information you gather from your product/service and market investigations, you should have a clear vision of your realistic target market. Here is an example of how this information is put together and conclusions are drawn. For more examples, go to www.salescoachpro.com.

Target Market Sample 1: Consumer Market

Item	Need	Want	Don't Need	Electronic
Logo	☐	☐	☐	☐
Business Cards	☐	☐	☐	☐
Brochure	☐	☐	☐	☐
Website	☐	☐	☐	☐
Newsletter	☐	☐	☐	☐
Catalogue	☐	☐	☐	☐
Advertisements	☐	☐	☐	☐
Flyers	☐	☐	☐	☐
Fridge Magnet	☐	☐	☐	☐
Branded Swag (pens, etc.)	☐	☐	☐	☐
Employee Clothing	☐	☐	☐	☐
Cloth Bags	☐	☐	☐	☐
Product Labels	☐	☐	☐	☐
Signage	☐	☐	☐	☐
Internal Templates (Fax Cover, Memo, etc.)	☐	☐	☐	☐
Email Signature	☐	☐	☐	☐

Blog	☐	☐	☐	☐
Letterhead + Envelopes	☐	☐	☐	☐
Thank You Cards	☐	☐	☐	☐
Notepads	☐	☐	☐	☐
Seasonal Gifts	☐	☐	☐	☐
Company Profile	☐	☐	☐	☐

Segmenting Your Market

Market segments are the groups within your target market, broken down by a determinant in one of the following four categories:

- demographics
- psychographics
- geographics
- behaviors

Segmenting your target market into several specific groups allows you to tailor your marketing campaign further and more specifically position your product or service. You may wish to divide your ad campaign into four sections. That way, you can target four specific markets with messages that will most resonate with a specific audience.

For example, a clothing store for babies may choose to segment its target market by psychographics or lifestyle. If the larger target market is married females between the ages of twenty-five and forty-five, with children under five, and an annual household income of at least $100,000, these can be broken down into the following lifestyle segments:

- fitness-oriented mothers
- career-oriented mothers
- new mothers

With these three categories, unique marketing messages can be created that speak to the hot buttons of each segment. The more accurate and specific you can make communications with your target market, the greater impact you will have on your revenues.

Market Segmentation Variables

Demographic	Psychographic	Geographic	Behavioristic
Age	Personality	Religion	Brand Loyalty
Income	Lifestyle	Country	Product Usage
Gender	Values	City	Purchase Frequency
Generation	Attitude	Area	Profitability
Nationality	Motivation	Neighbourhood	Readiness to Buy
Ethnicity	Activities	Density	User Status
Marital Status	Interests	Climate	
Family Size			
Occupation			
Religion			
Language			
Education			
Employment			
Type			
Housing Type			
Housing			
Ownership			
Political			
Affiliation			

Understanding Your Target Market

Once you have determined who makes up your target market, learn everything you can about them. You need to have a strong understanding of who they are, what they like, where they shop, why they buy, and how they spend their time. Remind yourself that you may *think* you know your market, but until you have verified the information, you'll be driving your marketing strategy blind.

Be aware that markets—just like people—change. Just because you knew your market when you started your business ten years ago, it doesn't mean you know it now. Regular market research is part of any successful business plan and a great habit to start.

Types of Market Research

Surveys

The simplest way to gather information from your clients or target market is through a survey. You can draft a questionnaire full of questions about your product, service, market demographics, buyer motivations, and so on. Anonymous surveys will produce the most accurate information, since names are not attached to the results or specific comments.

Depending on the purpose—whether it is to gather demographic information, product or service feedback, or other data—there are a number of ways to administer a survey.

1. Telephone

Telephone surveys are a more time-consuming option but have the benefit of live communication with your target market. To get the most honest feedback, it is generally best to have a third party conduct this type of survey. This is the method that market researchers use for polling, which is highly reliable.

2. Online

Online surveys are the easiest to administer yourself. There are many web-based services that quickly and easily allow to you customize your survey and send it to your e-mail marketing list. These services can also analyze, summarize, and interpret the results. Keep in mind that the results include only those who are motivated to respond, which may slant your results.

3. Paper Based

Paper surveys are seldom used and can prove to be an inefficient methodology. Like online surveys, your results are based on the feedback of those who were motivated to respond. The time and effort involved in taking the survey and returning it to your place of business may deter people from participating.

Keep in mind that surveys can be complex to administer and consume more time and resources than you have planned. If you have the budget, consider hiring a professional market research firm to lead or assist in the process. This will also ensure the methodology is standard practice and will garner the most accurate results.

Website Analysis

Tracking your website traffic is an excellent way to research your existing and potential customers' interests and behaviors. From this information, you can ensure the design, structure, and content of your website caters to the people who use it and the people you want to use it.

User-friendly website traffic analytic programs can easily show you who is visiting your site, where they are from, and what pages of your site they are viewing. Services like Google Analytics can tell you what page they arrive at, where they click to, how much time they spend on each page, and from which page they leave the site.

This is powerful (and free!) information to have in your market research, and it is easy to monitor monthly or weekly, depending on the needs of your business.

Customer Purchase Data (Consumer Behavior)

If you do not have the budget to conduct your own professional market research, you can use existing resources on consumer behavior. While this data may not be specific to your region or city, general consumer research is actual data that can be helpful in confirming assumptions you may have about your target market.

Your customer loyalty program of your point-of-sale system may also be of help in tracking customer purchases and identifying trends in purchase behavior. If you can track who is buying, what they're buying, and how often they're buying, you'll have an arsenal of powerful insight into your existing client base.

Focus Groups

Focus groups look at the psychographic and behavioristic aspects of your target market. Groups of six to twelve people are gathered and asked general and specific questions about their purchase motivations and behaviors. These questions could relate to your business in particular or to the general industry.

Focus group sessions can also be time consuming to organize and facilitate, so consider hiring the services of a professional market research firm. You may also receive more honest information if a third party is asking the questions and receiving the responses from focus group participants.

For cost savings, consider partnering with an associate in the same industry, but who is not a direct competitor, and who would benefit from the same market data.

4

Creating Effective Marketing Material

Your marketing material is sent out in the world to do one thing: act as an ambassador for your product or service. This may seem like a big job for a piece of paper, but it's a helpful way to think about the materials you create.

When you meet with a potential or existing client, you do a number of things. You dress appropriately. You make sure you are well prepared, with all the information customers could need. You anticipate their needs and offer a solution to their problems. You may also provide that information according to client preference.

Chances are, you wouldn't meet with clients just for the sake of meeting with a client—say, for instance, to show off your new suit. Likewise, you shouldn't create and distribute nonessential materials. We all know that one of the biggest challenges for small businesses is the limited number of zeros attached to their marketing budget. Marketing materials can be expensive, and a single, well-produced piece has the ability to devour the entire budget. Given that billion-dollar marketing campaigns fail every day, how can you be sure to make the most of, and be successful with, your limited dollars?

The answer? Limit yourself to only the essential items for your individual business and produce them well with existing resources.

Your Essential Marketing Materials

The easiest way to throw away your marketing budget is to create and produce marketing materials you don't need. Since many pieces of ad copy are paper based, this not only leaves you with boxes of extra (outdated) materials. It also takes a huge toll on the environment. Take some time to determine what marketing materials you do need, and stick to that list. It's easy to want to "keep up with the Joneses" when your competition comes out with a new piece, but your focus should be on attracting and retaining a customer base, not matching the competition item for item.

Know your target market. Make sure you have a solid understanding of your customer base. From that knowledge, you can easily determine the best way to reach out and communicate with them. Are they a paper-based or techno savvy client group? Do they appreciate being contacted by e-mail or regular mail? Are they impressed by flashy design or prefer simple pieces? How you communicate is often just as or more important that what you communicate.

Pay attention to costs. Do you really need a die-cut business card? Does your flyer absolutely require ink to the edges? Unique touches to marketing material can grab a customer's attention, but they can also dramatically increase the cost of production. Keep an eye out during the design process, and make strategic choices about graphic elements.

Make mistakes—in small batches. Not sure if that flyer is going to do the trick? Testing out a limited time offer? Small production runs may cost a little more, but you'll avoid collecting boxes of unusable materials. Or, try a split run with different versions of the same piece, and see what works best.

Keep the environment in mind. Environmental responsibility is on everyone's mind these days—including your customers. Always question if a particular marketing item can be produced in electronic format. Consider eliminating plastic bags in exchange for cloth ones printed with your logo, print everything double-sided, send electronic newsletters, use your website to communicate, and use recycled paper and envelopes when you can.

Brainstorm your wish list. Create a list of desired marketing materials and ignore expenses, clients, or any other constraint. Then, beside each item, indicate if it is a needed, wanted, not needed, or an electronic item. The next page includes a checklist to get you started. Once you have finished, rewrite your list in priority order. This will keep you focused on the essentials only.

Marketing Materials Checklist

Item	Need	Want	Don't Need	Electronic
Logo	☐	☐	☐	☐
Business Cards	☐	☐	☐	☐
Brochure	☐	☐	☐	☐
Website	☐	☐	☐	☐
Newsletter	☐	☐	☐	☐
Catalogue	☐	☐	☐	☐
Advertisements	☐	☐	☐	☐
Flyers	☐	☐	☐	☐
Fridge Magnet	☐	☐	☐	☐
Branded Swag (pens, etc.)	☐	☐	☐	☐
Employee Clothing	☐	☐	☐	☐
Cloth Bags	☐	☐	☐	☐
Product Labels	☐	☐	☐	☐
Signage	☐	☐	☐	☐
Internal Templates (Fax Cover, Memo, etc.)	☐	☐	☐	☐
Email Signature	☐	☐	☐	☐
Blog	☐	☐	☐	☐
Letterhead + Envelopes	☐	☐	☐	☐
Thank You Cards	☐	☐	☐	☐
Notepads	☐	☐	☐	☐
Seasonal Gifts	☐	☐	☐	☐
Company Profile	☐	☐	☐	☐

Headlines + Subheadlines

If the only thing your potential customers will identify you by is your headlines, how do you think your current marketing materials would fare? Headlines need to be bold, dramatic, shocking, and answer your clients' questions, "What's in it for me?" or, "Why should I care?"

Headlines (and sub headlines) are vital in today's market, because we are bombarded with so much information that we scan everything. Readers skim your materials to find out why they should pay attention to or consider your product or service. Use your headlines to hit their hot buttons, and tell them why they should care!

Remember that headlines and subhead lines are not just for advertisements. They work wonders in newsletters, sales letters, brochures, and websites. They can be incorporated into all of your essential marketing materials.

Design

The cost of professional design can quickly eat up most of your marketing budget. However, the cost of distributing materials that look and feel unprofessional can often be much higher. The key is to find the middle ground.

Unless you have design or desktop publishing experience—or even if you do—your time is probably not best spent designing your own marketing materials. Depending on the size of your business and your graphic needs (for example, do you need frequent photography of your products?), there are a number of options from which to choose:

1. *Hire a design agency.* This is no doubt the most costly of your options. However, if you have a number of items to be designed, you may be able to get a package rate. Another option is to have the design agency create a logo and stationery package for you, and then create a how-to guide for using the logo, fonts, and other graphic elements in the rest of your marketing materials.

2. *Hire a freelance designer.* For most small businesses, the benefits of using a freelance designer (aside from cost savings) are convenience and trust. If you are lucky enough to find one you work well with, establish a seamless working relationship and you'll never again worry about the design of your marketing materials. Ask colleagues for recommendations of local designers or post an ad on craigslist.

3. *Hire a part-time design employee.* Need to hire someone part time for a task around the office or shop? Consider recruiting someone with design skills and hiring them for part-time work. This could include graphic design students or someone with an interest (and talent) in the field. This is exactly what I did when needing to develop new brochures. I found a

43

student who understood the technology and had a design background. He was also able to critique and make better my website.

Whichever option you choose—or if you choose to design the materials yourself—the two most important things to remember about design are as follows:

1. *Keep it consistent.* Your marketing materials must be consistent, or your customers will never learn to recognize your brand.
2. *Keep it simple.* Simple, clean design is the most effective way of communicating. Use "wow" pieces sparingly.

Guidelines for the Top-10 Marketing Materials

Logo

- *Use design resources.* If you are going to spend any money on outside design help, this is the time to do it. Your logo is the visual representation of your product or service and appears on everything that relates to your business. This is the core of your brand image and needs to be done right the first time.
- *Remember the purpose.* Your logo needs to be a unique reflection of your business, business values, and the industry in which you work. Before you commit to your

logo, make sure to give careful consideration to color choice, image selection, and image recognition—as well as to logos that already exist in the marketplace. Get an outside opinion from your family and friends, and use their feedback.

- *Don't get too complicated.* Can it be produced and seen clearly in black and white? In a single color? With your company name? Too often, businesses design their own logos that include a complex assortment of photos, words, and solid design elements. These do not photocopy well and can't be clearly read when produced at a small scale. Keep your logo design down to a graphic image and the name of your business.

Business Cards

- *Cover the basics.* A business card needs to communicate your basic contact information to potential clients, including who you are and what your business does. Make sure you've covered the basics and made it easy for them to contact you.
- *Name*
- *Title*
- *Company Name*
- *Company Slogan/Description*
- *Phone Number*
- *E-mail Address*
- *Fax Number*
- *Address*
- *Cell Number (if applicable)*

- *Website*
- *Make it memorable.* Be creative. Choose interesting shapes, die-cuts, orientation (vertical vs. horizontal), bright colors, and unique materials (wood, plastic, magnet, aluminum, or foam). You don't have to go crazy or spend lots of money to do this. Simple, clever twists on basic design make an impact. Just keep it relevant to your product or service.
- *Give them a reason to keep it.* What is going to keep them from throwing it out or filing it in a three-inch binder of other cards? Make the card worth keeping by adding something useful to the backside. For example, some coffee shops put frequent buyer incentives on the backside of their cards, encouraging customers to keep them in their wallets. Other examples include pickup schedules, reminders, calendars, testimonials, or coupons.
- *Produce a high-quality card.* Use at least hundred-pound card stock, and print in color. Choose clear, easy to read fonts no smaller than nine points.

Letterhead

- *Ensure professional quality.* Letterhead that is simple, clean, and well produced allows the reader to focus on the important part: the content. Have your letterhead professionally printed on thirty-two-pound paper or choose a textured stock. Show you are invested in the professionalism of your company.

- *Pay attention to design choices.* The design of your marketing material should reflect your corporate values and the personality of your organization. If you are environmentally conscious, choose recycled paper and put that fact in small print at the bottom of the page. Letterhead can also be a place for subtle graphic elements, like watermarks, in addition to your logo.
- *Be consistent with other materials.* Your letterhead is part of your stationery package and should look and feel the same as the rest of your pieces. For example, if your business cards have been printed with rounded corners, so should your letterhead. Use consistent fonts, colors, and logo placement on your letterhead, business cards, fax cover sheets, and other internal documents to ensure recognition and ease of readability.

Brochures

- *Cover the basics.* Each of your brochures should include your basic marketing message and detailed company contact information. Product or service features and customer benefits should also be clearly displayed and described.
- *Stay focused on the brochure's purpose.* Why are you producing this brochure? Are you featuring a new product line? Trying to increase awareness? Introducing your service to a new market? Stay closely connected to the purpose behind your brochure, and

ensure all the information and images in the brochure support that purpose.

- *Keep it simple.* Make sure the design and information organization is clean and easy to navigate. Like advertisements, blank spaces give the reader a break and make it easier to focus on key messages.
- *Choose high-quality production.* If you don't invest in your business, why should anyone else? Produce your brochure on high-quality paper, in vivid color, and have it professionally folded. An impressive looking brochure will travel from one client's hands to another's.
- *Keep it fresh.* It you produce brochures on a regular basis, consider giving each a theme to distinguish the information as new and interesting. Keep the overall look and feel consistent, but play with images and content layout to revitalize the design.

Newsletters

- *Be in touch.* Don't wait until your existing clients walk back into your store. Show them they're important to your business, and keep them updated on new products and services by distributing a personalized newsletter.
- *Use an online distribution service.* Online e-mail marketing tools (Customer Relationship Management tools) have never been easier or less expensive to use. They enable you to personalize your letters without much effort. These services will also track which clients

open their newsletters and which click through to your website.

- *Provide information; tell a story.* Engage the reader with a short anecdote or a piece of relevant information. Many people are bombarded daily by hard-copy and electronic letters, so make sure yours is worthy of their reading time. Include an "experts corner" or "new product feature," and structure the newsletter like your own business newspaper. Add links to relevant media articles or special offers.

- *Choose a distribution frequency you can maintain.* Newsletters can be time consuming, so be realistic about how often you promise to distribute them. This depends on your resources and the needs of your business, but once a month to once every three months is generally a good time frame.

Company (or Corporate) Profile

- *Your ultimate company brochure.* Your company profile includes all pertinent information about your business and your offering, and acts as the basis for all other marketing items. These are generally longer pieces—from five to twenty pages in length—allowing you ample room for written and visual content.

- *Tell your story.* The company profile is the place to tell the story of your business. Engage the reader by using anecdotes, and describe how and why your company was created. If you inherited the family business, describe how you're carrying on tradition and instilling new life. If you created your company from scratch with your college roommate, let the reader know. These real-life details are interesting and establish trust with your potential clients and associates.

- *Communicate your values.* Here you have the space to describe your company's vision, values, approach, and philosophies. Make sure you relate your values to your offering, and keep this section short and succinct.

- *Explain your offering—features, benefits, and all.* Just like your brochure, make sure to describe the full features and benefits of your products or services. Sprinkle testimonials throughout the design to back up your statements. This can include your full range of services or simply be an overview of your product types. Use professional images and creative copy to keep readers engaged.

- *Choose high-quality design and production.* Spend time creating a company profile that will last. Then, spend money producing one that will impress. Choose glossy paper and a high-quality press. Leave the profiles around your store and office for clients to read and admire.

Signage

- *Get professional advice.* Outdoor signage can be a daunting task for anyone who hasn't designed, produced, or otherwise gone through the process.

Since signage is influenced by a variety of factors—one of which is your municipal government's signage laws—you may wish to enlist the help of a professional signage designer or printer to guide you through the process and avoid costly errors.

- *Make it visible.* Your outdoor signage should be easily seen from the street or within the plaza or complex in which you are located. In some cases, you may need more than one sign to do this. Keep in mind how your sign will look at night as well as during the day. Your company logo and phone number or website needs to be visible at all times.

- *Make it distinct.* When it comes to signage, you can get really creative with materials, lights, and colors. While you need to maintain logo, color, and font consistency, you can add other graphic elements—including three-dimensional elements and window treatments—that may not work on the rest of your marketing materials. Make your signage memorable.

- *Remember your indoor signage.* Every business needs indoor signage to remind customers where they are. This includes section signage, product signage, map systems, and promotion announcements. If your business is located in an office, consider signage with your logo and company name above the reception area. Again, keep this signage consistent with the rest of your company materials, and you will be contributing to brand recognition.

Advertisements + Flyers

- *Place ads strategically.* Once you have determined who your target market is, you need to focus on advertising in publications they are most likely to read and distributing flyers to places they are most likely to be. Spend ad dollars strategically, and don't spend them all at once. Take time to test what publications work, and which don't, by measuring the response from each placement. And when you place ads, request placement that is in the top right-hand corner.

- *Grab their attention.* You have less than half a second to grab the attention of your audience with print advertising, so use it wisely. Spend the bulk of your time crafting the headline and choosing compelling images.

- *Keep their attention.* If you caught their attention, you have another two seconds to keep it. Use subheadings to entice them to read on for the details of your product or service.

- *Tell them why they should buy.* Always include your marketing message in your advertising. Describe the features and benefits of your product or service, but focus on the benefits that will trigger an emotional response from your target audience: love, money, luxury, convenience, and security.

- *Tell them how they can buy.* Include a call to action beside your contact information, and include your phone number, website address, and business address (if applicable). You may wish to include a scarcity or urgency offer to compel your readers to act fast.

- *Know the importance of white space.* If you try to cram too much information into your ad or flyer, your readers will skip it. Clean, clear, easy to read ads and one-page flyers with succinct messages are most effective.

Website

- *Be purpose focused.* Like your brochure, your website can serve a number of purposes. To be effective, you need to narrow in on the specific purpose when designing the content structure of the pages. Who is your audience? What do you want them to know when they leave the site? What do you want the site to make them do? Visit your store? Buy your offering? Pick up the phone? Make sure you are clear on this point before you start.
- *Make the address easy to find and remember.* A website address that is too long or too complicated will not be found or remembered. Do a search for available website addresses that relate to your business or marketing message, and try to secure a site with a .com ending. If your company name is taken, use a guarantee instead.
- *Focus on content.* The overall structure of how you organize the content on your site is like the foundation of your house. You can change the paint color and the furniture, but the foundation is more or less there for

good. Before you work with a designer and create the visual fabric of your website, focus on creating solid, clearly organized copy. Put together a map of your structure, starting with your home page and subpages, and allocate specific content to each page.

- *Revitalize regularly.* Your company is always changing, and so should your website. This is an important—and relatively inexpensive—way to communicate your company news and achievements and most likely, the easiest accessed source of information for your current and potential customers. Have areas for easy content updates, like a "news" section. Make sure sections like "employees" and "services" are kept up to date. For larger updates, go back to your purpose and website map, and make sure the content changes still support the original intent of the website.

- *Organize for intuition.* Make key information, especially your contact information, easy to access. You can quickly tell if a website is easy to navigate, because the information you are looking for appears in a natural order. For example, when visiting a restaurant website, a link to the reservations page is provided on the menu page. While you're putting together your website map, do some online research and investigate what does and doesn't work. A good rule of thumb is to ensure it takes no more than three clicks to access a page. Bury content too deeply, and your audience will get frustrated and leave.

- *Keep consistent with marketing materials.* Your website is an extension of your marketing campaign and should be treated as such. Use consistent logo placements, fonts, colors, and images so all elements of your materials are unified. The same is true for marketing campaigns. If you are running a new promotion or featuring a new item in an advertisement, include same information on your website. Customers responding to the ad will be reinforced, and customers who did not see the ad, but visit your website, will be aware of the offer.

- *Measure your results.* Your website is a piece of your marketing materials, just like brochures and advertisements, and should be evaluated for effectiveness on a regular basis. Easy website analysis tools, like Google Analytics, will show you which pages your audience is viewing, how long they're staying on each page, and where and when they leave the site. That is powerful information when it comes to structuring content and choosing on which page to put your most important messages.

5

Advertising for Immediate Profits

Why do you advertise?

Seems like a silly question, doesn't it? Placing ads in newspapers and on radio or television seems like a no-brainer way of growing or maintaining your business. You let a group of people know where your business is and what you sell, and you'll always have customers dropping by. Right?

It's a little more complicated than that. There's your powerful offer, your strong guarantee, the placement of your headline, and how you structure your body copy. But what I'm really trying to pin down is *why* you chose to place that ad. What is the specific purpose for each advertisement you send out into the world?

Without a solid purpose or strategy behind every advertisement, it is impossible to measure what is and is not working. If you placed an ad offering two for one shampoo one week, and sales for conditioner skyrocketed, would you consider your ad successful? Absolutely not. Sales might have gone up, but the reason you placed the ad was to increase sales on shampoo, which didn't happen.

The point is that each advertising dollar should be spent with purpose, focused on a desired outcome, and relevant to the big picture. Advertising is expensive! What's the point of spending money on advertising unless you're making your money back and then some?

Types of Advertising

There are endless options when it comes to choosing which media on which to advertise. The media is a broad and complicated industry, with highly segmented readership. This can help and hurt your advertising efforts. You have access to highly targeted audiences, but you may also spend a great deal of money on advertising your target market doesn't go near.

What follows are the major types of media advertising.

Print

Print is the most common form of advertising. Ad production is relatively easy and straightforward, and placement is less expensive than broadcast advertising. We'll be focusing on this form of advertising in detail later in the chapter.

Types of print media:

newspapers—daily and weekly
magazines
trade journals
newsletters

Radio

Local radio advertising reaches a broad audience within a geographic area. Satellite/Internet radio will offer you a wider audience and could be very effective if you want to reach a National audience. This form of advertising can be highly profitable for some businesses and utterly useless for others. Always consider if there is a simpler, less-expensive way of getting your message to your target audience.

Key points to consider for radio advertising:

use of sounds, voices, tones
length
gaining listener's attention
call to action

Television

Television advertising is largely out reach for most small-business budgets. Creating, developing, and producing TV spots is a costly endeavor and does not always generate an acceptable return on investment.

This form of advertising generally reaches a broad audience, depending on the time slot the ad airs. Typically, the most expensive airspace is during the region's most popular 6 o'clock news program, or prime time (6 p.m. to 10 p.m.) television lineup.

There are some cost-effective alternatives to TV advertising that you can implement online. You could create a promotional video for your company, and post it on your website and YouTube or Facebook, or play it in your store. Be creative with your ad budget when it comes to broadcast.

Online

Online advertising has emerged as an effective tool for your marketing efforts. Internet usage has dramatically increased, and usage patterns have become easier to identify. This form of advertising also allows you to reach a highly qualified audience with minimal investment in ad creation.

Places to advertise online:

Facebook
Google Adwords
online media (online newspapers and broadcast stations)
Craigslist
banner ads on complementary websites

Classified Ads

Classified advertising is one of the most highly targeted and cost-effective choices you can make in your overall strategy. People who read classifieds have typically made a decision to buy something and are looking for places to do so. This is also a great way to test your headlines, offer, and guarantee before you invest in higher-priced advertising.

Classified ad types:

daily and weekly newspapers
online
trade journals

Specific tips for effective classified ads:

- Pick a format for your ad within the specifications of the publication. Will it look like a print display ad? A semi-display ad? A classic line ad? This will affect how you structure your message.
- Choose the category—or two—that best fits with what you have to offer. If two apply, place an ad in both, and measure which category generated more leads.
- Grab the attention of your reader with a killer headline and then list benefits, make an irresistible offer, and offer a strong guarantee. Keep the layout simple, and ensure the font size is easy to read.
- Notice how other companies create their ads, and do something to stand out. The classifieds page is

typically cluttered and full of text, so you will need to distinguish your business in some way.

- Use standard abbreviations when creating line ads to maintain consistency. Ask the ad department for a list of abbreviations it typically uses.

Niche

Niche advertising can take any of the forms previously discussed. The advantage of niche advertising is the super-segmentation of each outlet's audience. Typically, there is a very small market in each niche, and a single publication that caters to it. This is very effective for companies who have no need for broad market advertising in traditional or mainstream publication.

Types of niche advertising:

trade journals
alternative media
blogs
internal communications: newsletters, and so on

Your Advertising Strategy

Develop a Purpose-Driven Strategy

Know exactly why you are choosing to advertise, as well as the objective of each and every ad. Compare the benefits of advertising to other promotional strategies, like media relations, direct mail, referral strategies, and customer loyalty programs.

Some common objectives for advertising strategies include the following:

- generate qualified leads
- increase sales
- promote new products or services
- position products or services
- increase business awareness
- maintain business awareness
- complement existing promotional strategies

These objectives will dictate where you advertise, the size of each advertisement, and how often you advertise in each outlet.

Find Your Target Audience

Before you do anything, get a solid handle on who makes up your target market and each of the segments within it. Think about demographic factors, like age, sex, location, and occupation, as well as behavioral factors like spending motivations and habits. The composition of your target audience will be the deciding factor when choosing which media to advertise with and what to say in each of the advertisements.

Decide on a Frequency

The frequency of your advertising campaign will depend on a number of factors, including budget, purpose, outlet, results, and timing. You may wish to publish a weekly ad that includes a coupon in your local paper. Or, you may only need to advertise a few times a year, just before your peak seasons.

Establish an advertising schedule for the year, or at least each quarter, and plan each advertisement in advance. This will ensure you are not scrambling to place an ad at the last minute and that each ad is part of an overall proactive strategy instead of a reactive one.

Choose Your Outlets

Decide where you are going to advertise and how often in each outlet. You may wish to choose a variety of media to reach several target audiences, or just a large daily newspaper where the greatest number of people will see it.

When starting a new campaign, it is a good idea to test its effectiveness in smaller, less-expensive publications. Based on the results, you can make changes to the ad and place it in the more-expensive outlets.

Remember that although budget is a large factor when deciding on advertising media, it is entirely possible to implement a successful ad campaign with minimal financial investment. The key is to make sure each dollar you spend is carefully thought through, and your ads are placed in publications that reach your ideal customers.

Maximize Your Ad Costs with Bulk Purchases

If you plan to advertise in a specific publication several times within a given period, you will benefit from a meeting with the sales representative to review your needs. Media outlets will often offer discounted rates for multiple placements.

Remember that one company may own several media outlets, including TV, radio, and online media. Ask your sales rep for other discount opportunities when advertising within the ownership group.

Remember to Test and Measure

How will you know if your campaign is successful if you don't test and measure the results? The only true mistake you can make in advertising is neglecting to track and analyze the results each ad generates.

Get in the habit of keeping a copy of each ad, and record all the details of the placement, including publication, cost, date, response rate, and conversion rate. Many publications will mail you a clipping of your advertisement with your account statement, but don't rely on this as a clipping service.

Evaluate the effectiveness of each ad you place, and learn from what isn't working. If you are advertising in several outlets, make sure asking customers where they saw your ad as part of your incoming phone script and sales script. You will need to monitor not only what types of ads work the best but where the ads generate the highest response.

Creating Your Advertisement

You don't need to rely on professional copywriting or design assistance when crafting advertisements from your business. Spend your time and resources on what you are saying, and ensure the "how you say it" is clear, clean, and easy to read.

Ad Copy

Headlines

- Take at least half of the time you spend creating your ad to focus on the headline. Your headline will be the difference between your ad getting read—or not. Boldface your headlines for impact.
- You have about five seconds to grab the reader's attention, so create a headline that sparks curiosity, communicates benefits, or states something unbelievable. You can review the headlines section in the "Copywriting" chapter of my coaching website, www.salescoachpro.com.

Sub-Headlines

- The purpose of your sub-headline is to elaborate on your headline and convince the audience to read the body copy. All the rules of headline writing apply. If you did not mention benefits in your headline, do it in your sub-headline. Clearly tell the reader what is "in it" for him or her and get the person to read further.

Body Copy

- Choose your words wisely: you don't have room for lengthy paragraphs. Whenever possible, use bullet points to convey benefits, and keep your sentences short. You typically only have about forty-five words to convince the customer to keep reading.
- Always include your contact information—phone number and website address at the very least. This seems obvious, but can be forgotten in the design process.

Ad Layout

Size

- Choose your ad size based on the purpose of the ad and the budget you have available. Larger ads are more expensive, but you do need enough space to communicate your key message to the audience.

- If you place regular ads to maintain a presence in the local paper, you likely don't need full ad pages. Alternately, if you are launching a new product or service or having a blowout sale, you will want to buy more space to increase the potential impact.

Graphics

- Graphics should comprise about 25 percent of your total ad space, or more if you have a small amount of copy. Avoid drawings and clip art. Photographs will generate a better response. Don't underestimate the importance of white space. Give the reader space to "rest" their eyes between headlines and body copy paragraphs.

Font

- Choose clean fonts that are easy to read. Times New Roman and Arial are effective, simple choices. If you use two fonts in your advertisement, make sure you do not combine serif and sans serif fonts, and you keep consistency among headers and body copy.
- Ensure none of your copy is smaller than nine points. Your audience won't take the time or spend the effort to read tiny copy.

6

Using Scripts to Increase Sales Immediately

What do playbooks, prompts, guides, and scripts have in common? *They are popular tools that dictate or guide human behavior toward a desired outcome.*

Playbooks help coaches tell sports teams specifically how to play the game to overcome an opponent. Prompts help kick-start writers and other creative professionals when stuck in a rut. Guides provide a series of instructions so a person or team can complete or implement a specific task. Film scripts tell actors how to act in a particular role.

If you're in the business of sales, you also know about sales scripts. Sales scripts are tools that guide salespeople during interactions or conversations with potential customers. A large number of businesses use scripts as a way of to maintain consistency among a sales team, to train new salespeople, or to enhance sales skills. They may have a single script, or several; they may change their scripts regularly, or use the same one for years.

What most businesses overlook, however, is that the sales script is a living, breathing, changing member of their sales team. They may be internal documents, but they deserve just as much time and effort as your marketing materials.

Do You Really Need a Script?

The short answer is yes. You absolutely need a script for every customer interaction you and your salespeople may encounter. Sure, countless business owners and salespeople work every day without a script. If you own your own business, chances are you're already a pretty good salesperson. But if you are not using scripts, you're only working at half of your true potential—or half of your potential earnings.

They act as a map for your sales process, and provide prompts to trigger your memory and keep you on track. How many times have you made a cold call that didn't work out the way you wanted? Scripts dramatically improve the effectiveness and efficiency of your sales processes. A comprehensive set of scripts will also keep a level of consistency among your salespeople and the customer service they provide your clients.

Scripts don't have to be "cheesy" or read verbatim. Once scripts are written, memorized, and rehearsed, they become like film scripts: salespeople can breathe their own life and personality into the conversation, while staying focused on the call's objectives.

Why Your Scripts Aren't Working

If you a currently using scripts in your business, are they working? Are they as effective as they could be? How do you know? When was the last time they were reviewed or updated?

Scripts are like any other element of your marketing campaign: they need to be tested and measured for results, and changed based on what is or is not working. Measure the success of your script based on your conversion rates. Of all the people you speak to and with whom the script is used, how many are being converted from leads to sales?

When evaluating your existing scripts, ask yourself the following questions:

How old is this script? For what was it written? Scripts are living, breathing members of your company. They need to be written and rewritten and rewritten again as the needs of your customers change, your product or services change, or as new strategies are implemented.

Does this script address all the customer objections we regularly hear? Every time you hear a customer raise an objection that is not included on the script, add it. The power of your script lies in the ability to anticipate customer concerns and answer them before they're raised.

Does this script sound the same as the others? Your scripts are part of the package that represents you as a company. There should be a consistent feel or approach throughout your scripts that your customers will recognize and be confident dealing with.

Is everyone using the script? Who on your team regularly uses these scripts? Just the junior staff? Only the top-performing staff? Make sure everyone is singing from the same song sheet, and your customers will appreciate the consistency.

Types of Scripts

Depending on the product or service you offer and the marketing strategies you have chosen, there are countless types of scripts you can prepare for your business. When you sit down to create your scripts, start by making a list of all the instances when you and your staff members interact with your existing or potential customers. Then, prioritize the list from most to least important, and start writing from the top. Here are some commonly used scripts and their purposes:

Sales Presentation Script

Each time you or your sales staff makes a presentation, the same or a slightly modified version of the same script should be used. This script will include sample icebreakers, a presentation on benefits and features of the product or service, and a list of possible objections and responses. These scripts should help alleviate some of the nervousness or anxiety associated with public speaking.

Closing Script

Closing scripts help you do just that: close the sale. This could include a list of closing prompts or statements to get the transaction started. This type of script also includes a list of possible customer objections and planned responses.

Incoming Phone Call Script

Everyone who calls your business should be treated the same way; consistent information should be gathered and provided to the customer. In the initial greeting, the person answering the phone should state the company name, department name, and his or her own name. This goes for the main line and each individual or department extension.

Cold-Call Script

This is one of the most important scripts you can perfect for your business. The cold-call script must master the art of quickly getting the attention of the customer and then engaging and persuading them with the benefits of the product or service. The caller needs to use open-ended questions to establish common ground with the potential customer and find a way to get him or her to talk about the individual's needs.

Direct Mail Follow-Up Script

Scripts for outgoing calls intended to follow up on a direct mail piece are essential for every direct mail campaign. These follow-ups are designed to call qualified leads who have already received information and an offer, and convert them into customers. These scripts should focus on enticing customers to act and overcoming any objections that may have prevented them from acting sooner.

Market Research Script

Scripts used primarily for the purpose of gathering information should be designed to get the customer to talk. A focus on open-ended questions and relationship-building statements will help relax the customer and encourage honest dialogue.

Difficult Customer Script

Just like every salesperson needs to practice the sales process, you and your staff need to practice the ability to handle difficult customers. If you operate a retail business, this is especially important, as difficult customers often present themselves in front of other customers. These scripts should help you diffuse the situation, calm the customer, and then handle the person's objections.

David L. McKimmy

Creating Scripts

Creating powerful scripts is not complicated, but it will take some time to complete. Focus on the most vital scripts for your business first, and engage the assistance of your sales staff in drafting or reviewing the scripts.

Your Script Binder

Keep master copies of all of your scripts in one organized place. An effective way to do this is to create a binder, and use tabs to separate each type of script.

You will also want to create a separate tab for customer objections, and list every single customer objection you have ever heard in relation to your product or service. Find a way to organize each objection, so you can easily find them; for example, group them by category or separate them with tabs. Then, list your responses next to each objection. Create several responses to each objection, with different customer types in mind. A master list of customer objections and responses is an invaluable tool for any business owner, salesperson, and script writer. The more responses you can think of, the better.

Remember, the script binder is never "finished." You will need to make sure it is updated and added to on a regular basis.

Writing Scripts—Step by Step

Step One: Record What You're Doing Now

If you aren't using scripts—or even if you are—start by recording yourself in action. Use video or audio recording to tape yourself on the phone, in a sales presentation, or with a customer. Make notes about your body language, word choice, customer reaction and body language, responses to objections, and closing statements.

You may also wish to ask an associate to make notes on your performance and discuss them with you in a constructive fashion.

Step Two: Evaluate What You're Doing Wrong

Take a look at your notes, and ask yourself the following questions:

- Ø How are you engaging the customer?
- Ø Are you building common ground and trust?
- Ø Does what you are saying matter to the customer?
- Ø Is your offer a powerful one?
- Ø What objections are raised?
- Ø How are you dealing with them?
- Ø What objections are you avoiding?
- Ø How natural is your close?
- Ø Are you as effective as you think you can be?

Once you have answered and made notes in response to these questions, make a list of things you need to improve and how you might go about doing so. Do you need to strengthen your closing statements? Do you need to brainstorm more responses to objections? Remember that everyone's script and sales process can be improved.

Step Three: Decide for Whom the Script Is Intended

So, now that you know the elements of your script you need to work on, you can begin drafting your new script or revising an old one. The first part of writing a script—or any piece of marketing material—is to have a strong understanding of for whom you are writing. Who is your target audience? What does your ideal customer look like? Consider demographic characteristics like age, sex, location, income, occupation, and marital status. Be as specific as possible. What are their purchase patterns? What motivates them to spend money?

If you are writing a cold-call script, you will need to develop or purchase a list of people who fall into the target market specifics you have established. If you are writing a sales script for in-store customers, spend some time reviewing what types of customers find their way into your place of business.

You will want to use words your target audience will not only understand but relate to and resonate with. Use sensory language that will trigger emotional and feeling responses: "I need this," "This will solve that problem," "I'll feel better if I have this," and so on.

Step Four: Decide What You Want to Say

There are typically five sections of every script. There may be more, depending on the type and purpose of script:

1. *Engage*
   - Get their attention or pique their interest.
   - Establish common ground.
   - Build trust, be human.
   - Ask for their time.

2. *Ask + Qualify*
   - Take control of the conversation by asking questions.
   - Focus on open-ended questions; that is, ones that cannot be answered with simply a yes or no.
   - Get the customer to talk.
   - Ask as many questions as you need to get information about the customer's needs and purchase motivations.

3. *Get Agreement*
   - Ask closed-ended questions to which you are sure the customer will respond with yes.
   - Get the customer to agree on the benefits of the product or service.
   - Repeat key points back to the customer to gain agreement.

4. *Overcome Objections*
   - Anticipate objections based on customer comments and then refute them.
   - Make informative assumptions about the customer's thought process, identify with his or her concern, and then refute it by using your own experiences.
   - Repeat concerns back to the customer to let him or her know you heard them.
   - Before you close, ask about any remaining objections.

5. *Close*
   - Assume you have overcome all objections and have the sale.
   - Ask the customer transactional questions, like delivery timing and payment method.
   - Be as confident and natural as possible.

Step Five: Train Your Staff

Once you have written your company's scripts, you will need to ensure your staff understand and are comfortable using them. Consider having a team meeting, and use role play to review each of the scripts. This will encourage your salespeople to practice among themselves and strengthen their sales skills. Ask them for feedback on the scripts, and make any necessary changes.

You will also need to decide how comfortable you are having your salespeople personalize the scripts to suit their own styles. Be clear what elements of the script are "company standards" and essential techniques, but also be flexible with your team.

Step Six: Continually Revise

After you have carefully crafted your script, put it to the test. Practice on your colleagues, friends, and family. Get their feedback, and make changes.

Remember that scripts will need to change and evolve as your business changes and evolves, and new products or services are introduced. Keep your script binder on your desk at all times, and continually make changes and improvements to it.

You may also wish to record and evaluate your performance on a regular basis. This is an exercise you could incorporate into regular employee reviews to use as a constructive tool for staff development.

Script Tips

- Practice anticipating and eliciting real objections, including ones your customer doesn't want to raise.
- Make the script yours. It should look, feel, and sound like you naturally do, not like you're reading off the page.
- Spend time with the masters. If there is a salesperson you admire in your community, ask to observe him or

her in action. Take notes on the person's performance and the techniques he or she uses for success.

- If your script is not successful, ask the customer why it is not. Even if you don't get the sale, you'll get a new objection you can craft responses to and never be stumped by it again.
- Don't fear objections. Just spend time identifying as many as possible and then practice overcoming them.
- Never stop thinking of responses to customer objections. Each objection could potentially have thirty responses geared toward specific customer types.
- Anecdotes are persuasive writing tools, so use them in your scripts. People enjoy hearing stories, especially ones that relate to them and their experiences, frustrations, and troubles. Let the story sell your product or service for you.
- Include body language in your scripts; it's just as important as your words. Try mimicking your subject's posture, arm position, and seating position. This has proved to create ease and build trust. However, take care to do so subtly, so the customer does not get the impression you are mocking him or her.
- If you only have your voice, use it. Pay attention to tone, language choice, speed, and background noise. You only have sound to establish a trusting relationships, so do it carefully.
- Be confident, and focus on a positive stream of self-talk to prepare for the call or presentation. Confidence sells.

- Spend time on your closing scripts, as they are a critical component of your presentation or phone call. This can be a challenging part of the sales process, so practice, practice, practice.

7

Profiting from Internet Marketing

Is your business online? If not, it should be.

The Internet is today's primary consumer research tool. (Forrester Research, July 2009) If your business does not have an online presence, it is harder for customers to find and choose your business over the competition. With over 73 percent of North Americans online, and estimated to grow to 82% by 2014, (Forrester Research, July 2009) it is no wonder individuals and businesses in all industries are looking to the Internet to enhance their marketing strategies.

Luckily, it has never been easier to establish and maintain a comprehensive online presence. Internet marketing—also referred to as online marketing, online advertising, or e-marketing—is a the fastest-growing medium for marketing. (Forrester Research, July 2009) But it is not just company websites that users are viewing. Blogs, consumer reviews, chat rooms, and a variety of social media are growing rapidly in popularity.

Used strategically and effectively, the Internet is a very powerful tool for businesses. It can be a cost-saving alternative to traditional marketing approaches and may be the most effective way to communicate with your target consumer.

A major advantage for a business with an Internet presence is the ability to be open at all times. Users can access your business twenty-four hours a day, seven days a week, and depending on your business and the purpose of the website, visitors can also purchase goods at any time.

Internet Marketing for Everyone

The Internet is a great way to create product and brand awareness, develop relationships with consumers, and share and exchange information. You can't afford not to take advantage of online marketing opportunities, because your competition is likely already there.

Internet marketing can take many forms. By creating and maintaining a website for your business, you are reaching out to a new consumer base. You can have full control over the messages users receive, and your business message has a global reach.

Internet marketing can be very cost effective. If you have an e-mail database of your customers, an e-newsletter may be cheaper and more effective than posted mail. You can deliver time-sensitive materials immediately and update your subscriber list instantaneously.

1. Yahoo.com
2. Google.com
3. YouTube
4. Windows Live
5. Facebook
6. MSN.com
7. Bing
8. Wikipedia
9. Blogger.com
10. Yahoo Japan

You will notice that half of these websites are search engines. An increasing number of consumers first research products, services, and companies online, whether it be to compare products, complete a sale, or look for a future employer. Most people in the 18-35 age group obtain all of their information online, including news, weather, and product research. The remaining sites are interactive sites, where users can upload information for social networking or information sharing.

Internet Marketing Strategies

Like all other elements of your marketing campaign, internet marketing needs to have clear goals and objectives. Creating brand and product awareness will not happen overnight, so it is important to budget accordingly to ensure there is money set aside for maintenance of the website and analytics.

Be flexible with ideas and options. Do your research first, try out different options, and test and measure the results. Metrics and evaluations should be monitored regularly and can be updated almost immediately. By keeping an eye out for what online marketing strategies are working and which are not, it will be easier to create a balanced portfolio of marketing techniques. You might find that in certain geographical areas, some marketing strategies are more effective than others.

The following recommendations are by no means the full extent of options available for marketing online, but it is a good place to start when deciding which ones are best suited to your company.

Create a Website

One major use for the Internet is information seeking, so you should provide consumers with firsthand information about your company. You have control over your branding and messaging and can also collect visitor information to determine what type of Internet user's access your website.

Search Engine Optimization

Since search engines comprise a large percent of the most visited sites globally, you can go through your website to make it more search engine friendly, with the aim of increasing your organic search listing. An organic search listing refers to listings in search engine results that appear in order or relevance to the entered search terms. You may wish to repeat key words throughout your website. When writing the copy for your site, keep the end reader in mind, of course, but also search engines.

When you design your website, remember search engines do not recognize any text that appears in Flash format. If your entire website is built on a Flash platform, you will have a poor organic search listing.

Price-per-Click Advertising

If you find visitors access your website after first searching for it through a search engine, it may be beneficial to advertise on these websites and bid on keywords associated with your company. These advertisements will appear at the top of the page or along the left side of the search results on a search engine. You can have control over the specific geographic area you wish to target, set a monthly budget, and have the option on only being charged when a user clicks on your link.

Online Directories

Listing your business in an online directory can be an inexpensive and effective online marketing strategy. However, you need to be able to distinguish your company from the plethora of competitors that may exist. You will likely need to complement this strategy with other brand awareness campaigns.

Online Ads (For Example, Banner Ads on Other Websites)

These advertisements can have positive or negative effects based on the reputation and consumer perception of the website on which you are advertising. These ads should be treated similarly to ads you place in local newspapers or other print publications.

Online Videos

With the growing popularity of sites such as YouTube, it is evident that people love researching online and being able to find video clips of the information they seek. Depending on your small business, you may want to upload informational videos or tutorials about your products or services.

Blogging

Blogging can be a fun and interactive way to communicate with users. A blog is traditionally a website maintained by an individual user that has regular entries, similar to a diary. These entries can be commentary, descriptions of events, pictures, videos, and more. Companies can use blogging as a way to keep users updated on current information and allow them to post comments. If blogging is something you wish to invest in, make sure it is regularly updated and monitored.

You may also provide products to bloggers in your industry to try and then review for their audience. You can find my blog at www.salescoachpro.com/blog.

Top-10 Mistakes to Avoid

Failure to Measure ROI

Which metrics are you using? Are your visitors actually motivated to purchase or sign up? If the benefits of your online campaign are not greater than the costs incurred, you may wish to reevaluate your Internet marketing strategy.

Poor Web Design

Poor Web design can leave a poor impression of your company on the visitor. It could result in frustration for visitors if they are not able to find easily what they went on your site to search for. It also does not build trust. If consumers do not trust your company or your website, you will not be able to complete the sale and develop a long-term relationship with that customer. You also need to include privacy protection and security when building trust.

You must ensure all information on the website is current and have customer service available if users experience difficulty or cannot find the information they seek. This could be as simple as providing a "Contact Us" e-mail or phone number for support.

Becoming Locked into an Advertising Strategy Early

Remember your marketing mix when creating a marketing strategy, and avoid putting all of your marketing eggs in one basket. Online marketing is a very valuable tool, but depending on your business and your target markets, other marketing campaigns may be better options for you. Especially if this is your first time to make a significant investment into your online sector, you want to remain flexible and able to adapt your strategy based on feedback received by researching and analyzing different options.

Acting Without Researching

Similar to becoming locked into an advertising strategy early, this mistake implies not dutifully testing and researching different online marketing options. For example, if your target consumer is sixty-five or older, and you are spending all of your marketing efforts into creating a blogging website (where the average ages of bloggers are between eighteen and thirty-five), you are likely not going to have a successful campaign.

Assuming More Visitors Mean More Sales

More visitors may not mean more sales if your website is used primarily for information and consumers purchase their products elsewhere. This is also true in reverse: you could have an increase in sales without an increase in unique visitors if your current consumer base is very loyal and willing to spend lots of money.

People will often collect information online about products they wish to purchase because it is easier to compare options, but they purchase in person. Even though shopping online is becoming quite popular, many people still prefer to see and feel the physical product before purchasing.

Failing to Follow Up with People Who Purchase

Repeat sales can account for a large percent of total revenue. It's no wonder organizations try to maintain loyal customers and may have customer relationship management systems in place. It is easier to get a happy customer to purchase again than it is to get a new customer to purchase once.

Failing to Incorporate Online Marketing into the Business Plan

By ensuring that your online marketing plan is fully integrated and accurately represents your organization's overall goals and objectives, the business plan will be more comprehensive and encompassing.

Trying to Discover Your Own Best Practices

It is very beneficial to use trial and error to determine the best online strategy for your company, but do not be afraid to do your research and learn from what others have already figured out. There will be many cases where someone was in a very similar position as you, and they may have some suggestions and secrets to share. Conducting research in advance can save a great deal of time and money.

Spending Too Much Too Fast

Although it may be cheaper than traditional marketing approaches, Internet marketing does have its costs. You have to consider the software and hardware designs, maintenance, distribution, supply chain management, and the time that will be required. You don't want to spend your entire marketing budget all at once.

Getting Distracted by Metrics that Are not Relevant

As discussed in the following section, there are endless reports and measurables you can analyze to determine the effectiveness of your campaign. You will need to establish which ones are actually relevant to your marketing.

Testing and Measuring Online

As with any element of your marketing campaign, you will need to track your results and measure them against your investment. Otherwise, how will you know if your online marketing is successful? These results—or metrics—need to be recorded and analyzed as to how they impact your overall return on investment (ROI).

Some examples of metrics are as follows:

- new account setups
- conversion rates
- page stickiness
- "contact us" form completion

Due to the popularity in online marketing and the importance of having a strong Web presence, companies have demanded more-sophisticated tracking tools and metrics for their online activities. It can be very difficult to know not only *what* to measure but also *how* to measure. Thankfully, it is easier than ever to get the information you need with the many types of software and services available, including Google Analytics, which are free and relatively accurate.

Eight Metrics to Track

The following are the key measurables to watch for when testing and measuring your Internet marketing efforts

Conversions

How many leads has your online presence generated, and of those leads, how many were turned into sales? Ultimately, your campaign needs to have a positive impact on your business.

Regardless of the specific purpose of the campaign—from lead generation and service sign-up to blog entries—you need to know how many customers are taking the desired action in response to your efforts. Your tracking tool will be able to provide you with this information.

Expenditures

If you are not making a profit—or at least breaking even—from your Internet marketing efforts, you need to change your strategy. Redistribute your financial resources, and reconsider your motives and objectives for your online campaign.

An easy way to do this analysis is to divide your total expenditures by conversions. This could also be broken down by product. You could also use a tracking tool and view reports on the "per visit value of every click" from every type of source. Your sources can include organic/search engine referrals, direct visit (i.e., person typed your Web address into their address bar), or e-mail/newsletter.

Attention

You need to keep a close eye on how much attention your website receives. One of the best ways to analyze this is to compare unique visitors to page views per visit to time onsite. How many people are visiting, how many pages are they viewing, what pages are they viewing, and how much time are they spending on the site?

A unique visitor is any person who visits the website in a given amount of time. For example, if Evelyn visits her online banking website daily for an entire month, over that one-month period, she is considered to be one unique visitor (not thirty visitors).

You may also want to incorporate referring sources as well: the places online that refer customers to your website. You'll be able to determine what referring sources offer the "best" visitors.

Top Referrals

Know who is doing the best job of referring clients to your website, and note how they are doing it. Is it the prominence of the link? Positioning? Reputation of the referring company?

Understanding where most of your visitors come from will allow you to focus on those types of sources when you increase your referral sites. They also allow you to gain a better understanding of your online market and target audience.

Bounce Rate

The bounce rate is the number of people who visit your home page but do not visit other pages. If you have a high bounce rate, you either have all the necessary information on your home page or you are not giving your customers a reason to click further.

In Google Analytics, the bounce rate is found under the "Content" or "Pages" report.

Errors

It is very important to track the errors visitors encounter while trying to access or view your website. For example, if someone links to your website, but makes a spelling error in typing the link, your user will see an error page in his or her browser and will not make it to your website. You may wish to buy the domains with common spelling mistakes, and link those addresses to your true home page. This will increase overall traffic and potential conversions.

Onsite Search Terms

If you have a "search website" function on your website, it is useful to monitor which terms users most frequently search. This can provide valuable insight into the user friendliness of your site and your website's navigation system. This information will be included in the traffic reporting tool.

Bailout Rates

If you provide users with the option to purchase something on your website (i.e., include a shopping cart), you can track where in the purchasing process people decided not to go through with the sale.

David L. McKimmy

This could be at the first step of receiving the order summary and total or when stating shipping options. By obtaining this information, a company can reorganize or revamp its website to make the sales process more fluid and, possibly, encourage more purchases.

Here are the three main questions you should be asking yourself when evaluating your website presence:

- Who visits my website?
- Where do visitors come from?
- Which pages are viewed?

8

Profiting from Direct Mail

This section shows you how to select your best prospects and create a suitable mailing piece for your campaign. It also discusses the importance of using a mailing list to select the most appropriate recipients for your direct mail.

The Benefits of Direct Mail Marketing

A direct mail campaign offers something of value to the recipient that persuades him or her to respond to it. Direct mail is a low-cost medium aimed at a select group or market, and it provides the following benefits:

- *accuracy*—allows you to target recipients geographically, demographically, and psycho graphically
- *efficiency*—enables you to analyze who responds to your advertising
- *flexibility*—allows you to conduct a wide variety of advertising and marketing tasks and offer samples of your produce/service
- *measurability*—gives you the advantage of testing each feature of your marketing strategy

- *accountability*—allows you to track results with a great degree of accuracy

Mailing Lists

A mailing list pinpoints prospects who are most likely to buy your products or services. You can create mailing lists from the following sources.

- internal
  people with whom you have dealt with in the past

- external—direct response list
  people who have responded in the past to your direct mail

- external—compiled list
  noncommercial databases, such as lists compiled by the government

Constructing a Mailing List

Use a basic database program to construct your mailing list. Enter all the details (customer name, address, contact details, and so on) as directed by the program, and save it under an easily identifiable name (for example, "Christmas discount offer mailing list"). This way, you can track exactly whom you have contacted for each of your direct mail campaigns.

Create Your Letter Using Your Usual Word Processing Program

Most word processing programs contain a mail merge feature. This allows you to write a single letter and address each copy and envelope individually with one command by accessing the mailing list you created with a database program.

Identifying Your Customer Base

Most businesses have what is known as the "80/20" sales base. This means that most sales come from a relatively small core of customers (in the above example, 20 percent). Knowing who your customers are is essential to maintaining and growing your business. By identifying your customers you can reach them through direct mail to make additional sales and secure customer loyalty.

Analyzing Your Customer Base

It is important to analyze information about the type of customers you attract and the traits they share. This will help you better understand your customers, target their interests and habits, and structure campaigns to which they are most likely to respond.

David L. McKimmy

Details to collect about your customer base include the following:

- name/address
- contact details (address, phone, e-mail)
- last purchase details (date, product, amount)
- how they found out about your business
- when they first purchased from you
- average spent per purchase
- frequency of purchases
- method of payment

Collecting Details

Collecting details about your customers can be achieved through the following methods:

- customer surveys
- customer detail forms
- customer mail-out service (for example, catalogs and newsletters)
- customer discount cards.

If you offer your customers something in return, they will happily fill in and return a simple questionnaire.

Tips for Writing a Direct Mail Piece

These tips will assist you in creating a direct mail piece.

1. *Start with a rough draft or plan.*

Jot down the main points you want to make. Don't worry too much about how it sounds. Ask yourself the following questions:

- What's my message?
- Who am I going to tell?
- What do I expect to happen?

Put the letter aside for a day or two. Then, look at it again with a fresh mind, and remove irrelevant information.

2. *Promote the benefits of your offer.*

Offer something of true value or benefit: for example, the product itself, the guarantee, a specific promise, a discounted price, or a free sample or trial.

3. *Use a conversational tone.*

Big words and long sentences will bore the reader. Single-line, punchy sentences are electric. Be friendly but not too familiar. Write as though you're writing to only one person.

4. *Keep it short.*

Make your offer clearly and succinctly. Your message will be lost in a long and cluttered letter.

5. *Write a personalized salutation.*

Address the customer by name, so the individual feels you are genuinely interested in him or her.

6. *Instruct the reader.*

Tell readers exactly what needs to be done to take advantage of your offer. For example, they must call your office within the next five days.

7. *Include a P.S.*

Everyone reads the P.S. on a letter. Use it to remind the reader of key aspects of your offer: for example, the time limit.

Response to Direct Mail

There are many aspects that can affect response to your direct mail. They include the following:

- the quality and accuracy of your mailing list
  Your mailing list might have been out of date, or you might have targeted the wrong clients for this particular campaign.

- your offer
  Your offer might not have been deemed valuable by the recipients.

- the timing of the piece
  Different times of the year will create different responses. For example, gift catalogs will be more successful at Christmas. Other seasonal issues should also be considered, such as the product's suitability to current weather conditions.

- the execution
  The format is important and can have a bearing on the result. The classic direct mail piece consists of a letter accompanied by a brochure.

Tracking the Effectiveness of Your Campaign

Always track the responses to your campaign so you can make adjustments as necessary. Note the following:

- how many letters you sent out
- the percentage of responses

- who responded
- the total number of sales resulting from the campaign
- the percentage of responses leading to sales
- who purchased

9

Doubling Your Referrals

Every business owner knows the cheapest and most effective form of advertising is positive word of mouth (WOM). This chapter looks at how to best generate WOM by proactively generating customer referrals. Referrals are the most powerful way for any business to grow. They are also the most effective and cost efficient way to generate new business.

In the majority of cases, most businesses already benefit from the power of WOM advertising. However, it is also important to establish proactive programs to generate customer referrals and to reward your customers for referring your business to others.

Benefits of Using Referrals to Grow Your Business

Some of the benefits of generating referrals in your business include the following:

- Save time: It is the most time-efficient way to generate business, as your clients do most of the work.

- Improves qualification: The lead is stronger, as the potential customer has a reference point when it comes to dealing with your organization.
- Rapport: It is easy to build rapport with a referred client, as you share common ground.
- Improve sales: The referral should be an easier sale, because they have "social proof" it is okay to buy from you because their friend already has.
- Saves money: You save money you would normally spend on other marketing initiatives.
- It's comfortable: People like recommending a business product or service if they have had a good experience.
- Recession proof: Referrals are a recession proof way of growing your business.

The Lost Opportunities of not Actively Generating Referrals

Maximizing every opportunity to grow your business should be "top of mind" for every business owner. By not actively generating referrals, you may be missing out on business that could easily come your way. People enjoy telling their friends and family when they have a good experience with a business. Therefore, it's really up to you to encourage your clients to promote your business.

Types of Referrals

There are three main ways in which customer referrals come to you business:

- passive WOM
- referrals at point of sale
- referrals from your existing clients

Passive WOM

Most businesses generate this type of referral. Assuming you have a satisfied customer base, your clients will, unbeknown to you, often refer others to your business. If your products and services are of exceptional standard, this will continue to happen.

Referrals at Point of Sale

The most difficult thing about referrals is actually asking for them. However, this should not be a problem if you have confidence in what you are selling. How you ask for them will depend on the type of business, product, and service. For example, if you are selling a high-ticket item, you may use a version of the following approach once the sale has been made:

> By the way, while I have you on the phone, could
> I ask you a favor? [Most people feel obliged if you

ask a favor of them.] I get a lot of my business through referrals from people like yourself. Do you know anyone—maybe a friend, relative, neighbor, or someone at work—who might be in the market for . . . [your product or service]?

The worst thing that can happen at this point is they will say no or won't feel comfortable nominating anyone. Like any type of prospecting, it's a numbers game. The more often you ask, the more often you will get leads to follow up.

Referrals from Existing Clients

This is a comfortable way to ask for referrals as it can be fairly nonintrusive, and clients generally feel more willing to refer business once they have trailed your products and services. A version of the previous script can be used or you can ask for referrals when surveying your clients. An example of a question you can ask in your survey to your customer base is:

Would you feel happy referring customers to our business?

_____

_____

_____

Once your survey has been conducted, you can follow up with a letter, such as the following, asking for referrals.

Your Logo   Your name

Your Address

Your Phone

Your Email Address

Date

Dear

Thank you for filling out the questionnaire we sent you on (date). We really appreciate your feedback and have since implemented new marketing, and service initiatives.

1. _____
2. _____
3. _____
4. _____

     (List all new initiatives introduced)

The reality is that most of our business comes from word of mouth/referrals from clients such as yourselves.

As a new initiative we want to direct our advertising budget back to our clients. That's why we are pleased to announce our new client referral program.

For every person you refer to us (once they become a client), you have the choice to receive a reward upon achieving the following levels:

1st sale generated—<A product/service that you supply>
2nd sale generated—$50 voucher to a store of choice, etc.

Example of Follow Up referral Sheet

Name of business: _____

Phone No. _____ Contact person: _____

Referred by: _____

Name of business: _____

Phone No. _____ Contact person: _____

Referred by: _____

Name of business: _____

Phone No. _____ Contact person: _____

Referred by: _____

Name of business: _____

Phone No. _____ Contact person: _____

Referred by: _____

Name of business: _____

Phone No. _____ Contact person: _____

Referred by: _____

Offering Incentives to Encourage Referrals

As a business owner, you may decide to offer incentives to encourage your clients to make referrals.

Types of Rewards

Offering rewards to the established client or the referral can work equally well. Examples of rewards include the following:

- Your products and services: This can be particularly successful, as you are able to provide these rewards at a wholesale cost.
- Discounts on future purchases: This encourages the clients to come back to you.
- Prizes and vouchers: These are easy to promote to clients.

Legal Implications

There are relevant laws that must be considered when it comes to referral selling. For example, by law, referrers must tell those to whom they recommend your business if they are being rewarded for doing so.

Keep in mind, though, that the better the offer and the better it is promoted, the more effective your referral program will be.

10

Creating Repeat Business and Developing Clients Who Pay, Stay, and Refer

When it comes to marketing and generating more income, most business owners are focused outward. They've carefully established and segmented their target market and created specific offers and messages for each market segment. They spend thousands of dollars in advertising and direct mail campaigns in hot pursuit of more leads, more customers, and more foot traffic. While this is an effective way to build a business, it is costly and time consuming. It requires constant and consistent effort, and while this approach does generate results, those results quickly disappear when the effort stops or becomes less intense.

Successful businesses with sustained growth have a double-edged marketing strategy. They focus their efforts outward—on new potential customers and marketing—as well as inward—on existing customers and referral business. These successful businesses have leveraged their existing efforts to generate more revenue. Simply put, their customers buy from them over and over again.

For most businesses, this is the easiest way to increase their revenues. Simple customer loyalty strategies and outstanding customer service are often all you need to dramatically increase sales by customers you already have.

The Cost of Your Customers

Do you know how much it costs your business to buy new customers? Each new customer who walks through your door—with the exception of referrals—has cost you money to acquire. You have spent money on advertising and promotions to generate leads and turn those leads into customers.

For example, if you placed an ad in your local newspaper for $1,000, and the ad brings in ten customers, you have paid $100 to acquire each customer. You would need to ensure each of those customers spent at least $200 to cover your margin and break even.

Alternately, if you spent two hours of your time and $10 per month on an e-mail marketing program to send a newsletter to your existing database of customers, and you bring in ten customers as a result, each customer has cost you $1.

Generating more repeat business means focusing on the marketing strategies that aim to keep your existing customers instead of purchasing new ones. This effectively reduces the cost of attracting new customers to your business.

These strategies are simple to implement and don't require much time investment. They only require a solid understanding of how to make customers want to come back and spend more of their money.

Keeping Your Customers

Marketing strategies that focus on keeping your current customer base are easy and enjoyable to implement. They allow you to build real relationships with the people you do business with, instead of dealing with a revolving door of people on the other end of your sales process.

Repeat customers create a community of people around your business who presumably share the same needs, desires, and frustrations. The information you gain from these customers (market research) can help you strengthen your understanding of your target audience and, more accurately, segment it.

Remember: The 80/20 rule: 80 percent of your revenue comes from 20 percent of your customers.(Pareto Principle, Wikipedia) Always focus on those customers. They are ideal customers you want to recruit and hold onto.

Customer Service: Make Them Love Buying from You

Every business—even those with excellent service standards—can improve the service they provide their customers. Customer service seems to be a dying concept in many businesses; more focus seems to be placed on the speed of the transaction. These days, you can even go to the grocery store and not speak to a single sales associate thanks to self-serve checkouts.

To improve your company's customer service standards, survey your customers and employees and brainstorm ways you can improve the experience of buying from your business.

Successful customer service—that which makes your customers buy from you—is

Consistent. The standards are kept by every person in your organization. Expectations are clear and followed through. Customers know what to expect and choose your business because of those expectations.

Convenient. It is nearly effortless for the customer to spend money at your place of business. Convenience can take many forms—location, product selection, value-added services like delivery—and it is also consistent.

Customer-driven. The service customers receive is exactly how they would like to be treated when buying your product or service. It is reflective of your target market and appropriate to your customers' lifestyle. Customers would probably not appreciate white linen tablecloths at a fast-food restaurant, but they would appreciate a two minutes or fewer guarantee.

Newsletters: Keep in Touch with Your Customers

A regular newsletter is an easy, time-effective, and inexpensive marketing strategy. Unfortunately, many small businesses think newsletters are too time consuming and too expensive to adopt as part of their marketing strategy.

The most popular type of newsletter distribution is via e-mail. This will cost your business as little at $10 per month for an e-mail marketing service subscription and can be customized to your unique branding. You may also do this in house and save the money.

Here is an easy, five-step process to starting a company newsletter.

1. *Pick your audience.* New customers? Market segment? Existing customers?
2. *Choose what you're going to say.* Company news? Feature product? New offer?
3. *Determine how you're going to say it.* Articles? Bullet points? Picture?
4. *Decide how it's going to get to your audience.* E-mail? Mail? In-store?
5. *Track your results.* How many people opened it? Read it? Took action?

Value-Added Service: Give Them Happy Surprises

Adding value to your business is an effective way of creating return customers. Every person I know would choose a mattress store that offered free delivery over one that did not. It's that simple.

There are many ways to add value to your business. Some methods are as follows:

- *Feature your expertise.* Use your knowledge to provide additional value to your customers. Offer a free consumer guide or report with every purchase.
- *Add convenience services.* Off a service that makes their purchase easier or more convenient. The best example of this is free shipping or delivery.
- *Package complementary services.* Packaging like items together creates an increase in perceived value. This is great for start-up kits.
- *Offer new products or services.* Feature top-of-the-line or exclusive products. Offer a new service or profile a new staff member with niche expertise.

Value-added services generate repeat customers in one of two ways:

1. *They impress customers on their first visit.* Impress your customers with great service, a product that meets their needs, and then wow them with something they weren't expecting. Get them to associate the

experience of dealing with your business with happy surprises, and create a perception of higher value.

2. *They entice customers to come back.* The introduction of a new value-added service can be enough to convince a customer to buy from you again. Their initial purchase established a trust and knowledge of your business and its processes. They will want to be included in anything new you have to offer, especially if there is exclusivity. It is easier to attract clients who have purchased from you than potential clients who have not.

Customer Loyalty Programs: Give Them Incentives

Another simple way to keep in touch with existing customers and keep them coming back to you is to create a customer loyalty program. These programs do not have to be complicated or costly and are relatively easy to maintain once they have been implemented. These programs also help you gain more information about your customers and their purchasing habits.

Here are some examples of simple loyalty programs that you can implement:

> *Free product or service.* Give customers every tenth (or sixth) product or service free. Produce stamp cards with your logo and contact information on it.

Reward dollars. Give customers a certain percentage of their purchase back in money that can only be spent in-store. Produce "funny money" with your logo and brand.

Reward points. Give them a certain number of points for every dollar they spend. These points can be spent in-store or on special items you bring in for points-only purchases.

Membership amenities. Give members access to VIP amenities unavailable to other customers. Produce member cards or give out member numbers.

Remember that for this strategy to work, you and your team have to understand and promote it. The program in itself becomes a product you sell.

Monetary Consideration

Give referring clients a preloaded debit card or gift card to a local restaurant. It would be even better if you knew referring client's favorite restaurant.

There are hundreds of ways to show your appreciation for referrals. Be creative and consistent.

So, What Do You Do From Here?

Take action! If you're already an accomplished business owner and earning in excess of $250,000.00 per year, use this book as direction to enhance the speed of your business success. If you are not as accomplished as you would like, the smartest thing to do is to concentrate on strategies to *learn,* and the *earn* will follow! If you are serious about taking the next step, go to work on yourself, study other business successes, and become a sponge for new and proven material. The amazing thing about the game of business is that when you put proven processes to work and continue to follow them, an abundance of success will follow. The biggest mistake is to start a process and then fall back into your old habits after a short time.

Above all, get the knowledge you need before you step onto the field. Think about it: if you were going to challenge Michael Jordan to a game of H-O-R-S-E for money, wouldn't it make sense to learn the game and practice before you stepped on the court to challenge him? It's amazing to me how many new, small-business owners start the game of business against seasoned professionals (the competition) without developing the necessary knowledge to be successful. Then they fail and blame the market, the economy, their location, and so on.

If you have a business and have not yet created wealth and systems that allow you to take time off, build retirement accounts, and pay for your children's college, learn and master the steps outlined in my book. I am a huge advocate of education and mentorships. Get the right information, find someone who knows how to walk you through them, and watch your quality of life take new shape.

For a free test drive of all my best tips, tricks, and marketing resources, visit www.SalesCoachPro.com. Follow my blog at salescoachpro.com/blog. There is also another book in the works, so keep an eye out for it. (Ahh . . . the value of marketing!)